NASCAR

The Greatest Races

written by Bob Woods

Reader's Digest
Children's Books

Pleasantville, New York • Montréal, Québec • Bath, United Kingdom

Copyright © 2004 NASCAR and Reader's Digest
Children's Publishing, Inc.
Published by Reader's Digest Children's Books
Reader's Digest Road, Pleasantville, NY U.S.A. 10570-7000
and Reader's Digest Children's Publishing Limited,
The Ice House, 124-126 Walcot Street, Bath UK BA1 5BG
Reader's Digest Children's Books is a trademark
and Reader's Digest is a registered trademark
of The Reader's Digest Association, Inc.
NASCAR® is a registered trademark of the
National Association for Stock Car Auto Racing, Inc.
All rights reserved. Manufactured in China.
Conforms to ASTM F963 and EN 71
10 9 8 7 6 5 4 3

Manuscript and consulting services provided by
Shoreline Publishing Group LLC.

Library of Congress Cataloging-in-Publication Data

Woods, Bob.
  NASCAR : the greatest races / written by Bob Woods.
     p. cm.
  ISBN 0-7944-0407-3
  1. NASCAR (Association)—History—Juvenile literature. 2. Stock car
racing—United States—History—Juvenile literature. 3. Automobile
racing drivers—United States—Biography—Juvenile literature. [1.
NASCAR (Association)—History. 2. Stock car racing—History. 3.
Automobile racing drivers.] I. Title: Greatest races. II. Title.
  GV1029.9.S74W67 2004
  796.72'0973—dc22
                                        2003067436

Contents

Introduction

What Makes a NASCAR Race Great?

The National Association for Stock Car Auto Racing—NASCAR—was founded in 1948. The following year, a rough-and-tumble band of daring drivers strapped on their helmets for the very first NASCAR race around a dirt track in North Carolina. In the 55 years since that historic event, literally thousands of stock car races have been run in small towns and large cities all across America.

For the drivers and their crews, officials, and loyal fans, each one of those races meant something special. The word "great" undoubtedly described countless wins, or near-wins, as well as the dedicated individuals behind the wheel or in the pits. But just as the cars and drivers are separated at the finish line by fast, faster, and fastest, there are great, greater, and greatest races.

Presented here is a selection of some of the

The crow's nest at Indianapolis Motor Speedway

greatest NASCAR events. Each one, from the first Daytona 500 in 1959 to the 2003 Carolina Dodge Dealers 400, recalls elements of greatness. There are tales of colorful drivers who fearlessly steered their machines through steep banked curves at 200 miles per hour (mph). There are stories of mad scrambles on the last lap with cars bumping and grinding to the checkered flag. There are times when the human eye can't quite see which neck-and-neck car has actually won, resulting in an always-thrilling photo finish.

There are fierce rivalries between guys who, off the track could be best friends—or even father and son. There are descriptions of bold strategies, risky maneuvers, and even downright trickery to navigate past the car ahead. Some moves don't work out exactly as planned, so there are accounts of crashes and pile-ups, too.

While a race's conclusion ultimately boils down to who drives the fastest car, other factors certainly contribute to its greatness. They might be human factors, like having the guts to attempt a seemingly impossible pass.

Every one of the tracks where NASCAR's premiere events are held is different. Some are a half-mile long, others more than two-and- a-half miles around. The ovals can be triangular or egg-shaped. Two of the tracks aren't even oval, but rather "road courses" that mix treacherous twists and turns with straightaways.

Taming different tracks requires various driving skills. Short tracks feature average speeds under 100 mph, yet constant shifting of gears, and tight turns. Superspeedways introduced the bumper-hugging technique known as "drafting," where the leader tows its follower in a wake of air. This typically sets up the so-called "slingshot" pass with the trailing car accelerating past the leader. (See page 32.) And then, of course, the roles are reversed and the chase goes back and forth.

There is one more essential ingredient. Actually, there are millions. They're the faithful and fanatical followers of NASCAR who pack the grandstands or watch on TV every weekend. They cheer their favorite driver and razz his rivals. They watch in wonder as these bold racers entertain them with remarkable talents and endless competitiveness.

For all these reasons, NASCAR has evolved into the most popular sport in the America. That means there's also no end in sight, no checkered flag or finish line, for more and more greatest races to come.

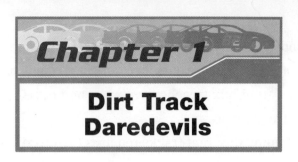

Chapter 1

Dirt Track Daredevils

Today's NASCAR fans are spoiled. They're used to seeing high-tech stock cars zooming around high-banked superspeedways at nearly 200 miles per hour. Millions of spectators turn out at the tracks every weekend to cheer on their favorite drivers, who are international superstars and earn millions of dollars. Every major race is broadcast live on national television. NASCAR has become the most popular spectator sport in America.

But this is not your grandparents' NASCAR. Back in 1948, when the first NASCAR races were run, the cars, the tracks, the drivers, and the fans were very different. Still, there was plenty of action, excitement, and hard-driving competition. Those rough-and-tumble races of the past would also pave the way for NASCAR's greatest races.

Of course, there's nothing new about auto racing itself. This exciting sport dates back more than a century, not too long after the gasoline-powered "horseless carriage" was patented in 1886 by Germany's Karl Friedrich Benz. In 1901, Henry Ford beat fellow automotive pioneer Alexander Winton in one of America's very first car races. It was held in Grosse Pointe, Michigan, outside of Detroit, known as the "Motor City" because that's where the auto industry began.

During the next three decades, better and faster cars came along. More races were run, and curious crowds of spectators showed up to watch. Most of the cars were specially built just for "flat-out" racing on long, straight-line courses. For example, the hard sand along Daytona Beach and Ormond Beach in Florida was perfect for high-speed competition. Daring drivers flocked to those sunny surf cities hoping to break land-speed records.

Gradually, everyday cars, like those seen driving down the street, got in on the action. They were called "stock," which means standard or typical. Stock car racing became popular, because people could easily relate to and enjoy watching cars just like theirs.

If cars could replace horses as a major mode of transportation, earlier racers thought: Why not borrow the concept of oval, dirt-covered horseracing tracks?

By the 1940s, oval dirt tracks hosted stock car races in small towns across the country. The young sport was particularly common in the Carolinas and Georgia.

Good ol' Southern boys climbed behind the wheels of stock cars with engines that had been "souped-up" to make them go faster. They developed their daredevil driving skills by racing on unpaved country roads. They would gossip and brag about who drove better or faster. Eventually, they settled the arguments by challenging each other in actual races at local dirt tracks. The races were set up by a growing number of small, semi-organized stock car racing associations. That situation would change with the arrival of Bill France on the scene.

William Henry Getty "Big Bill" France earned his nickname by virtue of standing six feet five inches tall and weighing 220 pounds. He moved to Daytona Beach, Florida, from Washington, D.C., in 1934. France was an auto mechanic with an itch for stock car racing.

France joined other hot rodders who put their gas pedals to the metal along Daytona's crude, 4.1-mile racetrack. It ran straight down the long, hard-sand beach, then looped around onto the pavement of Highway A1A. While fast and furious, those were loosely organized races with few rules and small crowds of spectators. Bill France had much greater plans—for Daytona and far beyond.

First, Big Bill organized drivers, race promoters, and various stock car officials into a single group that would oversee stock car racing throughout the country. On February 21, 1948, the National Association for Stock Car Auto Racing—NASCAR—was born, with France as its president.

NASCAR offered drivers hefty amounts of prize money and the chance to compete for a national championship. The big names in the sport then were Lee Petty, the Flock brothers (Tim, Fonty, and Bob), Curtis Turner, Buck Baker, Junior Johnson, Ned Jarrett, and Glenn "Fireball" Roberts. The first NASCAR champion was Red Byron, a World War II hero who raced a 1939 Ford. He had to have his left shoe bolted to the clutch pedal because an old war wound weakened his leg.

NASCAR's earliest races featured cars with souped-up, or "modified" engines. Those events were only moderately successful. The crowds weren't huge, and the races didn't receive much coverage in newspapers or sports magazines. One way to change that, Big Bill decided, was to ban modified cars and only allow "strictly stock" models. He was convinced that the public would identify with the sport more if drivers raced cars similar to their family sedans.

The first "strictly stock" NASCAR race was run on June 19, 1949, in Charlotte, North Carolina. It turned out to be a 150-mile thriller. A crowd of 13,000 fans packed the Charlotte Speedway's grandstands to witness history being made on the three-quarter mile dirt track. Thirty-three top drivers entered nine brands of cars: Buick, Cadillac, Chrysler, Ford, Hudson, Kaiser, Lincoln, Mercury, and Oldsmobile.

The cars circled the track for 200 laps, kicking up a thick cloud of dust. When it finally settled, Glenn Dunnaway appeared to have crossed the finish line first in a '47 Ford. His joy didn't last long, however. Race officials soon discovered that the car had illegal springs supporting its rear end. So Dunnaway was automatically disqualified. Jim Roper, whose 1949 Lincoln came in second, was declared the winner.

NASCAR racing changed dramatically on September 4, 1950, with the opening of the first paved oval, a 1.25-mile track in Darlington, South Carolina (since lengthened to 1.36 miles). It was also the first of stock car racing's "superspeedways." The track was wide enough for cars to race three across. It also

Lee Petty

featured treacherous, high-banked turns.

More than 20,000 spectators watched in awe as 75 cars started the Southern 500. (Today's NASCAR races only start 43 cars). The cars went faster on the asphalt track than on dirt tracks. But the higher speeds caused tires to wear out quicker. So drivers had to make more pit stops to put on new tires. Johnny Mantz solved that problem by putting heavier truck tires on his racer. The result was fewer pit stops—and a win!

NASCAR really took off after that. By 1955, it held 175 races at more than 50 different racetracks. In 1959, a spectacular new superspeedway opened in Daytona for the sport's most famous 500-mile race, the Daytona 500. More new tracks opened during the 1960s, the races became more exciting, and NASCAR became more popular.

Today's NASCAR consists of several series of races run at tracks all over the country. The major one is the NASCAR NEXTEL Cup Series, with 37 races held from February to November at 23 different tracks.

Nearly 7 million spectators attend NASCAR races each year. And even though it's no longer your grandparents' NASCAR, they're sure to love every minute of it now.

Not All Tracks Are Created Equal

Superspeedway

Technically, any track more than one mile long is a superspeedway. But the term is usually used to describe the high-banked ovals, such as Talladega and Daytona, where top speeds exceed 200 mph. Talladega Superspeedway in Alabama is NASCAR's longest and fastest track. Mark Martin turned in the fastest time there, 188.354 mph, in a 500-mile race on May 5, 1997.

Short Track

Short tracks measure less than a mile. The speeds at short tracks are about half those at superspeedways. The shorter distance also keeps cars running in tighter packs, which sometimes means more crashes. The .533-mile oval at Bristol, Tennessee, has the highest banking (36 degrees) in NASCAR.

Road Course

Road courses combine tricky twists and hairpin turns with long straightaways. There are only two road courses in the NASCAR NEXTEL Cup Series: the Watkins Glen track in upstate New York and Infineon (formerly Sears Point) Raceway in California's Sonoma Valley.

Where the Action Is

Tracks that host NASCAR NEXTEL Cup Series

Track	Length	Shape
Atlanta Motor Speedway	1.540 Miles	Oval
Bristol Motor Speedway	0.533 Mile	Oval
California Speedway	2.000 Miles	D-Shaped Oval
Chicago Motor Speedway	1.000 Mile	Oval
Darlington Raceway	1.366 Miles	Egg-Shaped Oval
Daytona International Speedway	2.500 Miles	Tri-Oval
Dover International Speedway	1.000 Mile	Oval
Homestead-Miami Speedway	1.500 Miles	Oval
Indianapolis Motor Speedway	2.500 Miles	Quad-Oval
Infineon Raceway	1.949 Miles	Road Course
Kansas Speedway	1.500 Miles	Tri-Oval

Track	Length	Shape
Las Vegas Motor Speedway	1.500 Miles	Oval
Lowe's Motor Speedway	1.500 Miles	Quad-Oval
Martinsville Speedway	0.526 Mile	Oval
Michigan International Speedway	2.000 Miles	D-Shaped Oval
New Hampshire International Speedway	1.058 Miles	Oval
North Carolina Speedway	1.017 Miles	Oval
Phoenix International Raceway	1.000 Mile	Oval
Pocono Raceway	2.500 Miles	Tri-Oval
Richmond International Raceway	0.750 Mile	D-Shaped Oval
Talladega Superspeedway	2.660 Miles	Tri-Oval
Texas Motor Speedway	1.500 Miles	Quad-Oval
Watkins Glen International	2.450 Miles	Road Course

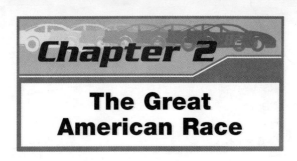

Chapter 2

The Great American Race

When Lee Petty and Johnny Beauchamp crossed the finish line at the 1959 Daytona 500, no one knew just how monumental that moment would be in NASCAR history. It was important because it was the very first 500-mile race at the brand-new, high-speed Daytona International Speedway. However, that fantastic finish would also become a shining example of what makes a NASCAR race great.

Petty's Oldsmobile 88 and Beauchamp's Ford Thunderbird streaked under the checkered flag side by side, fender to fender. They were so close, in fact, it took nearly three days to declare an official winner. Controversy, confusion, and anger surrounded the decision, but in the end, NASCAR would get it right when it declared Lee Petty the winner.

That 1959 Daytona 500—and a remarkable "Tiny" tale from the 1963 event—set the stage for what NASCAR fans have come to know as

"The Great American Race."

Today the Daytona 500 is the grandest race on NASCAR's busy annual calendar. It's what the Super Bowl is to the National Football League, the World Series is to Major League Baseball—except the 500 is the opening event of the NASCAR season, rather than the final one. Still, it's the race that every driver dreams of winning.

Actually, the inaugural race in '59 was a dream come true for "Big Bill" France. Ever since he founded NASCAR in 1948, France had imagined building the ultimate stock car racetrack in Daytona Beach. He realized that the city's Beach-Road Course was quickly becoming obsolete. Drivers wanted more superspeedways, like Darlington Raceway, where the cars went faster, the thrills soared higher, and the fans cheered louder. France also knew that a state-of-the-art track would help build NASCAR's popularity.

When Big Bill's dream track finally opened, it was a sight to behold. There was nothing quite like the Daytona International Speedway anywhere in the racing world—not even the famous Indianapolis Motor Speedway, home of the Indianapolis 500, could compare. Construction began in January 1959 at a site four miles from the Atlantic Ocean. It took nearly a year to build, at a cost of almost $2 million. The grandstands could hold 18,800 spectators, and portable bleachers could handle another 6,500. There was enough room inside the gigantic infield area to accommodate 75,000 more fans. There was parking for 35,000 cars.

Daytona's unique design was a tri-oval, with a triangular front stretch that allowed fans in the grandstands to see the entire track, as well as the pits. It measured 2.5 miles around, nearly twice the distance at Darlington (then 1.25 miles). The track's big turns were sloped, or banked, at an incredibly steep 31 degrees. Banking allows cars to go faster through turns without braking. They would go even faster as drivers learned the aerodynamics of drafting. That's when one speeding car trails right behind another, nose to tail. The two cars create a vacuum that pulls both cars along at a higher speed because there's less wind resistance.

Faster cars would also test the courage and skills of the men who drove them at Daytona. "There have been other tracks that separated the men from the boys," said driver Jimmy Thompson shortly before the first Daytona 500. "This is the track that will separate the brave from the weak after the boys are gone."

The 1959 Daytona 500

Sixty-four drivers started the race on the historic afternoon of February 22, 1959. With 15 laps left in the 200-lap event, it came down to a duel between Petty and Beauchamp. They changed leads five times before the white flag signaled one lap to go. As they rounded Turn 4, there was Joe Weatherly, a whole lap behind the leaders with no chance of winning. Still, Weatherly wouldn't move his Chevy out of their way, so they neared the finish line running three abreast. Weatherly was on the high side of the track, Petty in the middle, and Beauchamp at the bottom.

All three were driving white cars, which made it even more difficult for race officials to clearly see who crossed first. France agreed with the official starter that Beauchamp won by about a foot. Petty and his crew immediately disagreed. A poll of a dozen news reporters sided with Petty. Even as Beauchamp was being photographed with the trophy, an angry Petty was pleading his case to France. The NASCAR president finally decided to reconsider.

There were no official photo-finish cameras as there are today. So France had to rely on news photos and movies. Every shot showed Petty slightly ahead. "I'm sleeping good," Petty told the media during the ordeal, "'cause I know I had Beauchamp beat by about two feet."

France called Lee Petty almost 61 hours after the checkered flag had dropped to give him the good news that he indeed was the winner. Petty had averaged an amazing 135.521 mph in a race that featured 33 lead changes but not a single accident. Petty, whose son Richard would make NASCAR headlines soon, finished that 1959 season with his third points championship.

The exciting finish created plenty of positive buzz for NASCAR and the Daytona 500. The Cinderella story of the 1963 Great American Race would generate even more.

DeWayne Lund's nickname was "Tiny," even though he stood six feet four inches tall and weighed 270 pounds. He only won five major NASCAR races during his 21-year career (1955-75), though none bigger than the '63 Daytona 500. In 1963, Lund arrived in Daytona looking for a car to race, but then fate took him on a wild, unexpected ride.

Two weeks before the 500, fellow driver Marvin Panch was testing a Maserati-Ford sports car at the Speedway. He planned to race it in the upcoming 24 Hours of Daytona event. Lund watched in horror as the Maserati flipped and burst into flames. Tiny rushed to the accident scene and pulled Panch from the burning wreckage.

Panch was also scheduled to drive a Ford owned by the Wood Brothers team in the Daytona 500. But his injuries prevented him from racing. Instead, Panch convinced his hero, Lund, to take his place. Tiny came up big again.

Lund ran a smart race. He drafted behind several cars to save fuel. As a result, he made one less pit stop for gas. He saved more time by not changing tires at all. Lund took the checkered flag 24 seconds ahead of Fred Lorenzen in one of the most unexpected victories in NASCAR history. "I wanted to win for Marvin and for the Wood brothers because they took a chance," said Lund afterward. It turned out to be Tiny's chance of a lifetime.

Tiny Lund (right) celebrates his 1963 Daytona 500 win in Victory Lane.

Daytona's 10 Fastest Winners

Year	Champion	Car	Speed (MPH)
2001	Michael Waltrip	Chevy	182.555
1980	Buddy Baker	Olds	177.602
1987	Bill Elliott	Ford	176.263
1998	Dale Earnhardt	Chevy	172.712
1985	Bill Elliott	Ford	172.365
1981	Richard Petty	Buick	169.651
1992	Davey Allison	Ford	168.256
1990	Derrike Cope	Chevy	165.761
1999	Jeff Gordon	Chevy	161.551
1972	A. J. Foyt	Mercury	161.550

Chapter 3

Duel at Daytona

NASCAR drivers have great respect for one another, but that doesn't mean they let the other guys win! From its rough-and-tumble, dirt-track beginnings, NASCAR has always been about winning. It's driver versus driver, right to the end.

NASCAR fans are intensely loyal to their favorite drivers, and rivalries fuel those passions. There has probably never been a fiercer rivalry than the one between Richard Petty and David Pearson. They dueled throughout the 1960s and 1970s. Their greatest battle, however, commenced on February 15, 1976, at the 18th running of the Daytona 500. The dramatic conclusion is still considered one of the most exciting in NASCAR history.

Petty and Pearson came into the 1976 campaign as the top drivers of the day. Winning the season-opening Great American Race would be a feather in either driver's cap—in Richard Petty's case the familiar black cowboy hat. So both stock car superstars came to Florida ready to battle it out. That's just what they did, right down to the very last of the race's 200 laps.

With a huge crowd of 125,000 on their feet cheering, the white flag dropped. Millions more were watching at home on television as ABC-TV beamed live coverage of the final stages of the race. This was an important moment for NASCAR, as the sport was fairly new to national television. National television coverage plays a big role in boosting the popularity of the major sports leagues, and this broadcast was no exception. The auto racing fans who tuned in on this day saw an incredibly exciting race, one that set the stage for NASCAR's great leap forward on television.

After three hours of action-packed, back-and-forth driving, one lap remained. Petty clung to the lead, but just barely, with Pearson hugging his bumper in a classic drafting maneuver. Only a few inches separated the duo's speeding cars.

This type of knock-down, drag-out competition was nothing new to Petty and Pearson. Fans had grown accustomed to them chasing each other—and for good reason. Over the years, the pair finished 1–2, a NASCAR-record 63 times! Pearson wound up

David Pearson (No. 21) and Richard Petty (No. 43)
at the Daytona 500

holding a slight edge, winning 33 times compared to 30 victories for Petty. NASCAR journalist Bill Robinson once wrote, "What could be more beautiful than Petty and Pearson, side by side, flat out and belly to the ground, racing toward a hurrying sundown?"

The two drivers had plenty in common—superior driving talents and an intense desire to win races, among other things. Both were raised in small southern towns, where stock car racing was part of the culture. Both honed their skills on short dirt tracks. Yet their personal styles were vastly different.

Born in Level Cross, North Carolina, in 1937, Petty grew up in the shadow of his father, racing legend Lee Petty. Lee had started out as a farmer, but racing became the family business. Young Richard was around cars all the time, eventually becoming his dad's chief mechanic. "I'd go to school and then come home and work on race cars," Richard once told *Sports Illustrated* magazine.

Richard Petty was 20 years old when he entered NASCAR's top circuit, the Grand National, in 1958. He went on to become perhaps the greatest stock car driver of all time. But those early years had their rough moments, some at the hands of his dear old dad. In Richard's very first NASCAR Grand National event, Lee ran him into the wall and out of the race. Two years later, at Jacksonville Speedway Park, it appeared that Richard had won his first NASCAR race. But the second-place driver protested that Petty was at least a lap behind when he crossed the finish line. The officials checked it out, agreed, and awarded the win to that other driver—Lee Petty!

Richard enjoyed plenty of wins from that point on. Indeed, he retired in 1992 as the winningest driver in NASCAR history, with 200 victories to go along with seven points championships. In his record-setting 1967 season, Petty piled up an incredible 27 wins in 48 races, including 10 straight victories.

It's no wonder that Petty earned a regal nickname, "the King." Tall, handsome, and always in control, he was beloved by his subjects—millions of NASCAR fans. His big smile and friendly personality made him a media darling on and off the track.

David Pearson, born on December 22, 1940, in Whitney, South Carolina, motored onto the NASCAR scene in 1960. While quiet and reserved in public, like Petty, he made lots of noise behind the wheel of a race car. He earned rookie of the year honors his first season on the NASCAR Grand National circuit. Pearson might well have earned more than three

NASCAR championships had he raced more than five complete seasons during his 27-year career. Still, he started 574 races and won 105; he finished in the top five an incredible 52 percent of the time.

As Pearson piled up the checkered flags, he became well-known for his cunning driving style. He liked to lay back just behind the leaders, almost like playing possum, then crank it up in the latter stages of a race. That slyness, plus his prematurely gray hair, led folks to dub him the "Silver Fox."

Foxy to the finish in the '76 Daytona 500, Pearson executed a perfect slingshot pass to take the lead. A slingshot pass begins when one car is drafting right behind another car. As the front car speeds along, drafting creates a vacuum that pulls the rear car along at the same high speed as the front car. However, the rear car will go just as fast as the front car but the driver doesn't have to press the gas pedal as much. Since the rear car is running at less than full throttle, the trailing driver can hit the gas pedal and get an extra surge of power to shoot past the front car.

As Petty and Pearson approached Turn 3, Pearson gambled by riding "high on the bank." (High on the bank means close to the outside wall at the edge of the track. Low means closer to the infield.)

David Pearson (No. 21) limps to the finish ahead of Richard Petty (inset) in the 1976 Daytona 500.

Petty immediately went low to retake the lead. He did, but the two cars bumped, and moments later, they were both out of control.

Pearson's No. 21 Mercury hit the wall, then spun toward the infield, coming to a stop at the entrance of pit road. Petty's No. 43 Dodge careened into the wall, too, before sliding onto the grassy infield about 100 feet from the finish line.

Cool cat Pearson had kept his engine running by pressing the clutch pedal down during the crash. By depressing the clutch and disengaging the engine, Pearson prevented his car from stalling.

"Where's Richard?" he asked his crew over the radio. When they reported back that Petty was stalled out, "I took off as hard as I could," Pearson recalled after the race. It wasn't very hard—about 20 miles an hour—but it was enough to limp across the finish line first. Meanwhile, Petty's crew was frantically trying to push his car to the finish line. Even if that had worked, it was against NASCAR rules.

A few years ago, the King commented on coming that close to his seventh Daytona 500 win, which turned out to be Pearson's one and only victory in the event. "The race I'll be remembered most for," Petty said, "and the one I'll remember most, is the one I lost."

Sly Like a Fox

Petty and Pearson sparked their own fireworks at the end of the 1974 Firecracker 400 at Daytona. Pearson pulled a tricky move that solidified his reputation as the Silver Fox. The King once again found his rival to be a royal pain.

The scene that July 4 was one NASCAR fans had witnessed many times before. Pearson and Petty were running one-two in the final stages of the 160-lap race. With Petty hot on his tail as they began the final lap, Pearson knew that Petty would attempt to pass him with a slingshot maneuver.

As Petty jockeyed his STP Dodge into position, Pearson suddenly slowed down and steered toward the infield. Thinking Pearson's Purolator Mercury had run out of gas, Petty whizzed into the lead—but only for few seconds. To everyone's surprise, Pearson sped back up. Just as Petty realized that he'd been outfoxed, Pearson was drafting him. About a thousand feet from the finish line, Pearson completed a perfect slingshot pass to take the checkered flag.

"At the time, I was really mad," Petty said later. "But the longer we get away from it, the better David's move looks. I wish I had thought of it."

Petty vs. Pearson

Petty (1958–92)	Pearson (1960–86)
Starts 1,184	Starts 574
Wins 200	Wins 105
Poles 126	Poles 113
Championships 7	Championships 3

Chapter 4

Leader of
the Pack

The traffic can get pretty thick at Talladega
Superspeedway. Just ask Cale Yarborough. The crafty
veteran had to weave his way through major congestion
to win the heart-stopping 500-mile race there on May
6, 1984. In fact, the 40-car event featured an incredible
75 lead changes among 13 drivers before Yarborough
finally came out on top!

NASCAR president Big Bill France beamed like a
proud papa when Talladega opened in 1969. Originally
called Alabama International Motor Speedway, its
decade-old, tri-oval cousin in Daytona looked tame by
comparison. Talladega's steepest banked turns were
33 degrees, higher than at Daytona. At 2.66 miles, a bit
longer than Daytona's 2.50 miles, it was NASCAR's
longest course.

The combination of lengthy straightaways and
high banking created ideal conditions for drivers to hit
even higher speeds. Just before its debut, one reporter

wrote that, "the new track seemed sure to produce tire-frying, eye-bulging velocities well above 200 mph." So it came as no surprise when Talladega emerged as the sport's fastest venue, too.

The writer's estimate was right on target. Buddy Baker became the world's first stock car driver to break the 200-mph barrier on a closed course when he hit 200.477 mph while testing a car at Talladega on March 24, 1970. Twelve years later, Benny Parsons set a new qualifying lap record at 200.176 mph. Bill Elliott shattered that mark in 1987, clocking an incredible 212.809 mph during a qualifying lap.

Even the most daring stock car drivers felt the hair on the back of their necks stand up at those blazing speeds. So they welcomed NASCAR's required use of "restrictor plates" at Talladega and Daytona soon after Elliott's mad dash. A restrictor plate is attached to a car's engine to reduce the flow of air and fuel into its carburetor. That lowers horsepower and speed.

Restrictor plates led to a new NASCAR phenomenon—"pack racing." They forced cars to all run at about the same speed, which made drafting and slingshot passes a wise strategy. As a result, cars bunched up in packs, two or three across the wide

The 1984 Firecracker 400 with Richard Petty
in the lead

superspeedway track, like a high-speed wagon train. Throughout the race, drivers would slingshot past each other. Then, as the action came down to the final laps, clever maneuvering for the finish line took place.

Yarborough was no stranger to the peculiarities of superspeedways. He was born in 1939 in Sardis, South Carolina, not far from NASCAR's first paved oval in Darlington. As a kid, he hung around the track and developed a fascination with the cars and drivers. Yarborough competed in a soapbox derby at age 12, although he complained afterward to his mother that, "those cars just don't go fast enough." Before too long, he was cleaning up in stock car races at nearby dirt tracks. In 1957, he drove in his first NASCAR Grand National event, at Darlington no less—finishing a distant 42nd. Two years later, Yarborough became a full-timer. He would eventually become a superstar on NASCAR's top circuit and remain one for the next 30 seasons.

From 1959 to 1988, Yarborough started 559 races and won an impressive 83. He captured four Daytona 500 victories and won five Southern 500s, held at his old stomping ground, Darlington Speedway. He remains the only driver to win three consecutive NASCAR championships, from 1976–78.

The man who claims to have been bitten by a

rattlesnake, survived a lightning strike, wrestled alligators, and played semipro football was one tough cookie. Yarborough brought that same strong will to the racetrack every weekend. That was a good thing, because he'd need all he could muster that May afternoon in 1984 at Talladega.

The bumper-to-bumper drafting that day was as nerve-wracking as rush hour on a crowded highway. "It was amazing out there," Yarborough told reporters. "One second you'd be running first, then a couple seconds later a bunch of 'em drafted around and you'd be running tenth." Said fellow pack rat Benny Parsons, "It was the wildest race I've ever been in. Every time I got the lead, I immediately got shuffled back into the pack."

As the swarm of stock cars buzzed into the last lap of the race, Harry Gant held a narrow lead. A late bloomer on NASCAR's major circuit—a 39-year-old rookie in 1973—Gant had a tough-guy reputation, too. After Yarborough slipped past him on the backstretch to snatch the lead, Gant aimed to return the favor. Yet as he positioned his Chevy for a slingshot pass through the homestretch, a slower, lapped car blocked the way.

What Gant and the rest of the pack didn't know,

though, was that Yarborough's Chevy was running out of gas. "I barely made it to the finish line," he confessed. "I was running on fumes. Any further and Harry very likely would have beat me."

Gant, who came up two car lengths short, wasn't so sure. "Cale is a tough competitor," he said, "so I don't know if I could have gotten back by him. I'd sure have liked a clear shot, but traffic is part of racing and it was nobody's fault."

While those two were tangling for first and second place, a corps of NASCAR all-stars battled for third place. Jostling down the stretch were Bobby Allison, Baker, Parsons, and Petty. The first three crossed the finish line almost simultaneously, side by side by side. They were so close, officials had to review their photo-finish cameras before declaring who placed third. The final results for third through sixth place were Baker, Allison, Parsons, and Petty.

Yarborough had started the 188-lap race in the No. 1 pole position with a qualifying speed of 202.692 mph. His average speed for the race was a blistering 172.988 mph. "It was an interesting race," Allison told reporters, "because the speeds were way up there, but not a lot of people made mistakes." Such is the thrill of pack racing at Talladega.

The King's Crowning Moment

Richard Petty retired from racing in 1992 as the undisputed King of NASCAR. His 200 career wins are the most ever in the sport. Number two on the all-time list, his archrival David Pearson, is a distant 95 victories behind.

Considering all those wins, it's amazing that Petty's final one came in 1984 at the Pepsi Firecracker 400. The prolific driver who averaged nearly six wins per year beginning in 1958 went without a single one over his last eight seasons—a total of 227 races! That makes his 200th victory all the more memorable in the annals of NASCAR's greatest races.

It was the Fourth of July at Daytona International Speedway, where Petty had already posted nine wins, including seven Daytona 500s. Petty held a slight lead over Cale Yarborough with 20 laps left in the 160-lap event. As they began lap 158, Yarborough got into position for one of his patented slingshot passes. Suddenly, rookie driver Doug Heveron crashed, causing officials at the start-finish line to wave the yellow caution flag.

Under NASCAR's caution rules, cars remain on the track but have to slow down and can't pass. However, cars that have passed the flag stand before the yellow is waved can continue to speed around the track until they reach the start-finish line and have to slow down.

That was the case with Petty and Yarborough. Yarborough executed his slingshot and took the lead. Petty responded by pulling up right beside Yarborough, so close that their fenders actually bumped a few times. "The last 'bam' sort of squirted me ahead, giving me the slightest edge," Petty said after the race, explaining how he regained the lead for good.

Among those on hand to congratulate the King was President Ronald Reagan. "I'd been waiting for number 200 for an awfully long time," Petty said. "But it was worth the wait, the way it happened with the president being there and on July 4th. I couldn't have asked for a better time." And NASCAR couldn't have asked for a better race and champion.

NASCAR
Championship Series

Top 20 Career Wins Leaders
(as of 11/16/2003)

Driver	Wins	Driver	Wins
1. Richard Petty	200	11. Junior Johnson	50
2. David Pearson	105	12. Herb Thomas	48
3. Darrell Waltrip	84	13. Buck Baker	46
4. Bobby Allison	84	14. Bill Elliott*	44
5. Cale Yarborough	83	15. Tim Flock	40
6. Dale Earnhardt	76	16. Bobby Issac	37
7. Jeff Gordon*	64	17. Fireball Roberts	34
8. Lee Petty	54	18. Mark Martin*	33
9. Rusty Wallace*	54	19. Dale Jarrett*	31
10. Ned Jarrett	50	20. Rex White	28

* active driver

45

Chapter 5

Allison Wonderland

The short track in Bristol, Tennessee, is only about a half-mile around. However, the track has treated NASCAR fans to plenty of exciting, fender-bumping action since it opened in 1961. One of the most memorable events there was the finish of the 1990 Valleydale 500. In that famous race, Davey Allison won by about six inches ahead of runner-up Mark Martin. Allison had to overcome an accident early in the race, then made a gutsy move to come from behind and narrowly capture the checkered flag.

Navigating around Bristol Motor Speedway is no easy task, even for the most experienced stock car drivers. The .533-mile oval course's front and back straightaways are each only 650 feet long, so there's not much room to gain high speeds before braking and gearing down for the banked curves and turns. And, oh, those tight left turns! (All but two NASCAR races are run counter-clockwise, which means drivers only turn to the left.) Bristol boasts the steepest banking of any NASCAR track—36 degrees at its highest point in the turns. That makes steering through them extra tricky. Not only do drivers have to battle each other, but there's the downward pull of gravity to deal with, too. It takes tremendous strength and concentration to keep the race car steady. It's understandable, then, why fans at Bristol see more bumping and scraping than at the much longer superspeedway tracks.

Bristol remains one of NASCAR's favorite tracks, among spectators and drivers alike. It's a unique throwback to the dirt tracks that made the sport popular from its humble beginnings in the 1940s.

Bristol's backstretch area was reconstructed in the early 1990s to add more grandstand seating. Today the racetrack can accommodate more than 160,000 fans, up from 18,000 before the renovations. But like Wrigley, Fenway, and Yankee Stadium, the seats are close to the action. And because of the steep banks at Bristol, you can see the entire track, plus the pits, from any seat.

The fans at Bristol had plenty of racing activity to follow on April 8, 1990. There were some interesting stories among the field of 32 drivers. The lineup included old-timers, veterans in their prime, and up-and-coming young guns. The King, Richard Petty, was racing his familiar red, white, and blue No. 43, while his son Kyle piloted No. 42. Also at the starting line were Dale "The Intimidator" Earnhardt, Davey Allison, Bill Elliott, and Dale Jarrett, whose dad Ned was one of the television announcers for the race. Ned had won two championships during his storied NASCAR days, from 1953–66, before moving into a successful career in the broadcast booth.

Ned Jarrett and the rest of the TV crew were certainly keeping an eye on Davey Allison. Davey was a member of the so-called "Alabama Gang," a group of drivers from that southern state who made big names for themselves in stock car racing. Along with Neil Bonnett and Red Farmer, two generations of Allisons were members of the Alabama Gang. Davey's dad, Bobby, was the most successful, competing from 1961 to 1988. His 84 career victories ties him with Darrell Waltrip for third place on NASCAR's all-time wins list. Bobby won the points championship in 1983 and was voted Most Popular Driver six times. His younger brother Donnie only won 10 events on NASCAR's top circuit. But he took the checkered flag in more than 500 short-track races in other series.

Davey Allison in the lead at the 1990 Valleydale 500

Dale Earnhardt

No. 3, "The Intimidator," Dale Earnhardt

A NASCAR crew chief

Atlanta Motor Speedway

Kurt Busch

Jeff Gordon winning the 1999 Daytona 500,
followed by second-place finisher Dale Earnhardt

2003 NASCAR champion, Matt Kenseth

Bobby's sons Davey and Clifford both took to racing, though Davey enjoyed a longer and more successful career. In 1987, Davey became the first NASCAR rookie to qualify to start in the front row at the Daytona 500. He finished 27th, but went on to win two races that season and earned the rookie of the year honors. The following year, he came in second at Daytona by just two car lengths—behind his father! Davey finally captured his own checkered flag in the Great American Race in 1992.

Davey seemed destined to drive race cars. Legend has it that even before he could talk, he'd point at Daddy's racer and make engine noises. He got in trouble in grade school for drawing pictures of cars during class. Like so many young drivers, Davey started out on short tracks, with dreams of someday moving up to NASCAR's major series. His big break came in 1985, at age 24, when he started the Talladega 500 and finished in 10th place. He joined the circuit full-time in 1987, and went on to post 19 victories in 191 starts.

The Valleydale 500 at Bristol Motor Speedway was Allison's 94th career start, and it ended in dramatic fashion. He began in the 19th position, behind the wheel of his No. 28 Ford. He avoided serious damage from an accident in the early stages of the 500-lap (266.5-mile) race. However, the mishap left him deep in the middle of the pack. But he refused to give up hope of winning, so he and his crew decided to take a risk.

"We needed to get up front," Allison's team owner, Robert Yates, explained after the race. "There were 10 other cars on the lead lap, and we couldn't afford to be behind all of them. So we gambled on seeing what would happen if we didn't pit."

Allison's Ford Taurus had only 33 laps on its tires at that point. On the 391st lap of the race, when the leaders headed for pit road, Allison opted to stay on the track. The strategy proved to be brilliant. He took the lead and held it for the final 109 laps—but not without some rockin' and rollin' along the way from a couple of hard-driving challengers.

First there was Darrell Waltrip, who hugged Allison's bumper for 40 straight laps. Then a flat tire deflated Waltrip's hopes of overtaking the leader. That left Mark Martin as the only real threat. Their battle continued right down to the frantic final lap.

While Ricky Rudd and Sterling Marlin were tangling for third place, they bumped, sending Marlin into a spin. At the same time, Martin made his last

Bristol Motor Speedway

desperate move. He pulled his Ford out from behind Allison's car. The duo charged hard to the finish line, side by side. As the checkered flag dropped, the race was too close to call. Officials scrambled to review the videotape of the photo finish. Finally, they determined that Allison had won—by about the length of the smile on Allison's face as he hoisted his trophy.

"Unbelievable!" Allison beamed. "Mark got a good run going at me from the inside off Turn 4 and almost beat me." Said the runner-up, "I did all I could, but there just wasn't enough racetrack to get by Davey." That's the long and the short of it when NASCAR comes to the friendly confines of Bristol.

Father's and Son's Day

NASCAR is famous for being a family sport. And not just because Mom, Dad, and the kids come out to the races every weekend. There have been many famous families of drivers, too—the Pettys, Earnhardts, Jarretts, Waltrips, Bodines, and Labontes to name a few.

The 1988 Daytona 500 included an extra-special family theme. It's the only time in the history of the season-opening event that a father and son— Bobby and Davey Allison—finished first and second. However, the father-son duel almost didn't happen.

The 30th edition of the Great American Race was run on Valentine's Day, and it delivered a heart-pounding conclusion. With 14 laps to go, it appeared that Darrell Waltrip would be smothered with kisses in the winner's circle. Unfortunately, his engine went from sweet to sour and he dropped back to 10th place. That left the 50-year-old Allison daddy and his 24-year-old son to duke it out.

As they motored around Turn 3 on the final lap, Davey was so close to his father he practically had his Ford in Bobby's Buick's trunk. Davey dipped down to the inside of the track, pulling alongside Dad. "I saw

the nose of his car out of the corner of my eye," said Bobby during the post-race celebration. "But I was pretty sure my car had too many suds for him." Indeed, the bubble burst on Davey's boyhood fantasy of one day running 1–2 at Daytona with his famous father. "Since I was a kid, I'd dreamed about battling to the wire with my dad," Davey said after coming up two car lengths short. "The only difference was, I wanted him to finish second."

Tracking the Alabama Gang

All-Time Major Circuit Victories (1949–2001)

Bobby Allison	84
Davey Allison	19
Neil Bonnet	18
Donnie Allison	10

NASCAR Championships

Bobby Allison	1983

The 'Bama Boys at Bristol

Driver	Races	Wins	Finishes
Bobby Allison	44	4	23
Clifford Allison	3	0	0
Davey Allison	12	1	5
Donnie Allison	11	1	4
Neil Bonnet	19	0	3

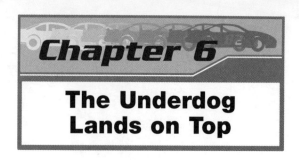

Chapter 6

The Underdog Lands on Top

At the 500-mile race at Atlanta Motor Speedway on November 15, 1992, so many amazing things happened that fans' heads must have been spinning as fast as the race cars' tires! There has never been a NASCAR race filled with so many surprising events happening at the same time:

- It was seven-time NASCAR champ Richard Petty's last race.
- It was future four-time champ Jeff Gordon's first race in NASCAR's major series.
- It was the first time that so many drivers— six—all started the last race of the season with a chance to win the points championship.
- In the end, it was Alan Kulwicki's first, and last, NASCAR title.

A number of bizarre twists and turns marked this nail-biter of a race at the track in Hampton, Georgia. Petty crashed and finished 35th. Gordon crashed and finished 31st. Davey Allison, the top contender for the season title, crashed and finished 27th. Bill Elliott won the race, but still ended up losing his big chance to take the lead in the season standings—by one measly lap!

Before the race, Alan Kulwicki was considered a huge underdog in the quest to win the NASCAR championship. However, underdogs are famous for their dogged determination. They never give up. They fight until the very end, no matter how great the odds are against them.

Alan Kulwicki began his NASCAR career in 1985. He was not your typical NASCAR driver back then. Unlike stars of the day such as Petty, Elliott, Allison, Dale Earnhardt Sr., and Darrell Waltrip, Kulwicki wasn't a good ol' boy from the South. Kulwicki hailed from Wisconsin, where he went to college and earned a degree in engineering. He also differed in wanting to own, build, and race his own cars, rather than depend on a team to do all the work for him. He removed the "Th" from the model name of his Ford Thunderbird to create an "Underbird." Kulwicki's stubbornness denied him the big bucks that come from deep-pocketed team owners and corporate sponsors. Still, he persevered.

Many of the other drivers kept an eye on Kulwicki.

They might have laughed at him for being different, but they respected him because he was a dedicated and talented driver. Everyone took notice after he joined the top NASCAR circuit full time in 1986 and captured the rookie of the year award. From 1987 until this 500-mile race in Atlanta, he racked up four wins and 35 top-five finishes.

So Kulwicki arrived at Atlanta Motor Speedway as a force to be reckoned with, as well as one of the six guys with a mathematical shot at the '92 title. Joining him in the chase to take the title were Allison, Elliott, Harry Gant, Mark Martin, and Kyle Petty. Allison was the points leader coming into the race. He needed only to finish sixth or better to clinch the title. Sure enough, on lap 253 of the 328-lap race, he was running sixth. Then a freak accident occurred. The car in front of him blew a tire, and the accident blew Allison's chances, and ended up finishing 27th. "It was a one in a hundred zillion chance you would have a problem," his car's disappointed owner, Robert Yates, said afterward.

That followed the fickle fate of the 55-year-old "King" Petty. This marked the last stop on the so-called Richard Petty Fan Appreciation Tour, the farewell for his final season. Before completing

Richard Petty

100 laps, he got in the middle of a pile-up that left his car in flames. "I went out in a blaze, but forgot the glory," joked Petty.

Was it simply coincidence that the soon-to-be crowned prince of NASCAR, Jeff Gordon, just 21, chose this race for his debut? Already a proven winner in NASCAR's Series and assured of joining the top circuit in 1993, Gordon didn't need to be there. "I was wondering if I had what it takes to be a winner in the series," he said after a crash into the wall on lap 164 took him out of action. ("What it takes to be a winner?" his fans might have asked. Gordon would prove he had more than enough to be a winner. By the end of 2003, he had collected more than 60 checkered flags and four championships.)

After Allison dropped out of contention, it became a two-man race between Elliott and Kulwicki. They swapped the lead several times during the second half of the race. The drama built as they chased the checkered flag, their minds no doubt on the $1 million prize for winning the championship.

Kulwicki was doing some other math in his head late in the race. He figured that to win the points title, he needed to remain in the lead for more laps than Elliott. It was all part of the intricate points formula

Jeff Gordon

used by NASCAR that season. Drivers earned points not only for where they finished in a race, but also for being in the lead. For leading any one lap, they earned five bonus points. The driver who led the most laps in the race earned 10 bonus points.

Knowing this, Kulwicki purposely made his final pit stop one lap after Elliott did. Although Elliott hung on to win the race, Kulwicki ended up leading one more lap during the race, thus earning 10 bonus points. When NASCAR officials added up both drivers' points for the entire season, Kulwicki took the title with those 10 points. It was the closest championship decision in NASCAR history. That created just one more angle to this complex race.

"I won, but I lost," said Elliott of the ironic results. Second-place finisher and new NASCAR champ Kulwicki could hardly believe his thrilling accomplishment. "It's like I'm living a dream," he said. "This is the answer to a long quest."

Unfortunately, that would be the greatest moment in Kulwicki's promising career. Less than a year later, the "underdog turned top dog" died in a private plane crash at age 38. However, Alan Kulwicki will always be remembered for the come-from-behind championship he earned on a crazy day in Atlanta.

1992 NASCAR Championships Final Standings

Driver	Points
1. Alan Kulwicki	4078
2. Bill Elliott	4068
3. Davey Allison	4015
4. Harry Gant	3955
5. Kyle Petty	3945
6. Mark Martin	3887
7. Ricky Rudd	3745
8. Terry Labonte	3674
9. Darrell Waltrip	3659
10. Sterling Marlin	3603

Chase for the Championship

Winning the NASCAR NEXTEL Cup Series championship is a little more complicated than just winning a single race. The season-long race for this title takes a lot of speed…and a lot of points! For 2004, NASCAR unveiled a new system for determining the overall champion. Here is how drivers earn points toward the NASCAR NEXTEL Cup Series championship.

The winning driver in each race gets 180 points (it used to be 175). The next five finishers (second through sixth) receive five points less in descending order (170, 165, 160, etc.) Positions seven through 11 are separated by four points (146, 142, etc.), while the rest of the field is separated by three points. Even finishing last (in 43rd place) earns a driver 34 points.

In addition, five bonus points are added for leading a lap and leading the most laps. The winning driver of a race can earn a maximum of 190 points. After each race, a driver's points are totaled up and added to his season total. Here's where the new wrinkle comes in for '04.

After the first 26 races, the top 10 drivers (plus any others within 400 points of the lead) will go into

a special "Chase for the Championship" group. Their points totals will be changed so that the leader has 5,050 points. Drivers following the leader will have five points less (5,045, 5,040, etc.). Then, the final 10 races of the season will be a tire-churning battle for the overall title.

Those 10 races will test every driver's skill. They'll race on long tracks, medium-length tracks, and short tracks. New tracks and older tracks will enjoy tastes of this end-of-the-season excitement.

What remains the same, however, is that the driver with the most points after the season's final race on November 21 in Miami will be the NASCAR NEXTEL Cup Series champion.

The payoff for all this hard work is pretty cool, too. The overall winner is guaranteed at least $5 million. Each of the other drivers in the final top 10 take home at least $1 million each.

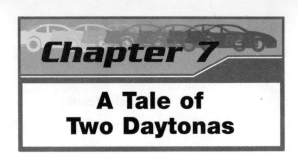

Chapter 7

A Tale of Two Daytonas

Dale Earnhardt stalked into the press conference following the 1998 Daytona 500. "The Intimidator," as the 46-year-old NASCAR legend was known, had been here before—19 times to be exact. This time, however, was entirely different.

"I'm here," he firmly announced to the huge crowd of reporters as he pulled a stuffed animal out from his driver's uniform, "and I've got that monkey off my back!" He slammed the toy monkey on the table. At long last, No. 3 had triumphed in the Great American Race!

Earnhardt wanted the whole world to know that the heavy burden of never having won NASCAR's most glamorous event, had finally been lifted from his shoulders. On his 20th attempt, at least, being runner-up was not an option for Earnhardt.

A year later, Earnhardt stood before the media horde once more. He was explaining yet another

Daytona International Speedway

second-place finish—his fifth in the Daytona 500—although this one had extra significance. He'd missed winning by an infinitesimal .128 seconds after attempting a last-ditch slingshot pass against leader Jeff Gordon, his young archrival.

There's no good explanation for the fact that an athlete can succeed tremendously sometimes and fail dramatically at others—especially at the most important moments. An all-star slugger can go hitless in the World Series. A quarterback with the best statistics during the regular season can flop in the Super Bowl. A can't-miss free-throw shooter can miss a game-winning shot in the championship final.

And Dale Earnhardt could have the most wins ever at the 2.5-mile track at Daytona International Speedway, except in the marquee event, the 500. Before February 15, 1998, Earnhardt had taken the checkered flag 30 times in various races at Daytona during his glorious 27-year career, but not once on the biggest day of the NASCAR season. He'd come oh-so-close several times, but just couldn't get the monkey—make that King Kong—off his back.

In 1986, he was leading the race, and then ran out of gas. Four years later, he sat in the lead with less than a lap to go when he cut a tire and dropped to

Dale Earnhardt winning the 1998 Daytona 500

fifth place. His car collided with a seagull head-on in 1991 and Dale saw his chance to win fly out the window. In 1993 and 1996, Dale Jarrett beat him on the last lap. After a mad dash in 1995, in which he made up 12 positions in the final 13 laps, Earnhardt finished second behind Sterling Marlin. Like Captain Ahab in the famous novel *Moby Dick*, would he ever catch his elusive white whale?

"The Man in Black"—another Earnhardt nickname, referring to the color he preferred in clothing and stock cars—was born to race, not chase whales. He was born on April 29, 1951, in Kannapolis, North Carolina, the heart of stock car country. His father, Ralph Earnhardt, was a NASCAR pioneer and winner of 250 short-track races. Dale joined NASCAR's premiere series full-time in 1979 and took rookie of the year honors. In 1980, he captured the first of his seven NASCAR championships, a record that would leave him tied with Richard Petty for most ever. He was the first driver to win top rookie and season champ honors in back-to-back seasons.

The 1998 Daytona 500 launched NASCAR's 50th anniversary and was the 40th running of its greatest race. What better stage could there be for the sport's top driver of his generation? Earnhardt's familiar

The 1999 Daytona 500 champion, Jeff Gordon

black Chevrolet Monte Carlo started in the number four position and moved to the head of the pack on lap 17 of the 200-lap event. Nearly every one of the more than 175,000 fans in attendance, regardless of their favorite driver, was pulling for No. 3.

Jeff Gordon was not. Representing the new generation of NASCAR drivers, raised on video games instead of dirt tracks, the 26-year-old "Boy Wonder" was Daytona's defending champion. Starting 29th, he jumped to the lead on lap 59 and appeared dominant. Then he experienced an Earnhardt moment, hitting a piece of debris that knocked his No. 24 Chevrolet out of whack.

The Intimidator regained the lead—and this year fate stayed on his side. He held off late challenges from Jeremy Mayfield, Rusty Wallace, Bobby Labonte, and Jeff Gordon. Gordon was out due to engine trouble on lap 198. On the next-to-last lap, three cars tangled, bringing out the yellow caution flags. All Earnhardt had to do was get back to the start-finish line first. He did, and the rest truly was history.

While the crowd roared, a touching scene played out along pit road as Earnhardt made his way to Victory Lane. Dozens of crew members from the other teams lined up to congratulate The Intimidator.

"We won it! We won it! We won it!" a jubilant Earnhardt yelled after spinning a few celebratory doughnuts in the infield grass. "The Daytona 500 is ours!"

The monkey had disappeared, but Earnhardt's young rival, Jeff Gordon, certainly would not. The two would again tussle in the Daytona 500's waning laps 12 months later.

At Daytona in 2000, Rusty Wallace's No. 2 Ford had been running strong all afternoon. Leading with 10 laps remaining, Wallace felt confident. Gordon felt daring. Wallace rode down low on the inside of the track. Gordon decided that the only way to pass him was to go even lower, onto the apron, the area right next to the infield. It was an extremely dangerous maneuver, especially at nearly 200 mph. Just behind him, Earnhardt watched and waited.

As Gordon made his bold move, Ricky Rudd suddenly pulled out of the pits and right into No. 24's path. In the blink of an eye, Gordon zigzagged, Wallace pulled back, and a nasty crash was avoided. "I had him pinned down there, but I wasn't going to try to wreck a bunch of cars," a disappointed Wallace said after the race. "I pulled up and he got me."

Another surprise came when Earnhardt then chose to draft inches behind rival Gordon instead of behind his good friend Wallace or teammate Mike Skinner. That actually helped Gordon, though he still had to fight off several slingshot pass attempts by No. 3 in the final laps.

"I thought he would have gone with the other two long before he went with me," Gordon said when later asked about The Intimidator's tactics. "But I think he knew he had a fast car and he could race with anybody. Maybe he wanted to race me for the finish."

He sure did, but came up a whisker short. "If I could have just gotten to him in the corners, I might have gotten under him and won," Earnhardt lamented. "But I couldn't get there. I got beat."

Two Champions: Head to Head

Daytona International Speedway hosts two big races during each NASCAR season. In February, the Daytona 500 kicks off the year. Around the Fourth of July, the Pepsi 400 is run. Here is how racing greats Dale Earnhardt Sr. and Jeff Gordon have gone head-to-head in their duels at Daytona.

Daytona 500

Dale Earnhardt

1993	2	1998	1
1994	7	1999	2
1995	2	2000	2
1996	2	2001	21
1997	31		

Jeff Gordon

1993	5	1998	16
1994	4	1999	1
1995	22	2000	34
1996	42	2001	30
1997	1		

Pepsi 400

Dale Earnhardt

1993	1	1997	4
1994	3	1998	10
1995	3	1999	2
1996	4	2000	8

Jeff Gordon

1993	5	1997	21
1994	8	1998	1
1995	1	1999	21
1996	3	2000	10

Daytona 500 Multiple Winners

Driver	Wins	Years
Richard Petty	7	1964, '66, '71, '73 '74, '79, '81
Cale Yarborough	4	1968, '77, '83, '84
Bobby Allison	3	1978, '82, '88
Dale Jarrett	3	1993, '96, 2000
Bill Elliott	2	1985, '87
Sterling Marlin	2	1994, '95
Jeff Gordon	2	1997, '99
Michael Waltrip	2	2001, '03

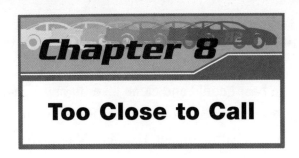

Chapter 8

Too Close to Call

As Ricky Craven crossed the finish line of the 2003 Carolina Dodge Dealers 400, he wasn't sure who had won. He and Kurt Busch had jostled over the final frantic two laps, and they were nose-to-nose when the checkered flag dropped. Craven finally realized he had captured his first race at famous Darlington Raceway moments later when he looked up at the scoring tower and saw his name on top.

"If we had lost that race, it would've been devastating," Craven said in his post-victory press conference. "It's exactly the kind of race that you want to win. It's exactly the kind of race that you don't want to lose."

It's also the type of race that could have gone either way. Craven's microscopic margin of victory was exactly .002 seconds (two thousandths of a second). By scant inches, it proved to be the closest call in NASCAR history. Said a disappointed, exhausted, yet still excited Busch, "It was awesome. That's what it's all about—racing as hard as you can. I drove [my] Ford the best I could and came up a bit shy, I guess."

It was totally appropriate for Darlington to host such an epic battle. In fact, that day, March 16, marked the 100th major NASCAR race at Darlington, the sport's very first paved oval. The granddaddy of superspeedways is renowned as the track that's "too tough to tame."

Darlington came by the nickname honestly. It was built in 1949 on a one-time cotton field by local businessman Harold Brasington. He actually hatched the idea for the racetrack while attending the 1933 Indianapolis 500. Folks thought he was crazy when he returned home and said he wanted to build an Indy-like, mile-and-a-quarter superspeedway smack dab in their tiny rural town. But Brasington had faith in the future of "Big Bill" France's new stock car racing association, so he plowed ahead.

The track's distinctive egg-shape design was not an accident. Sherman Ramsey, the man from whom Brasington bought the land, insisted that a minnow pond remain untouched. As a result, turns three and four on the west end are especially narrow and tricky to navigate. The area has become known as the

Ricky Craven

"Darlington stripe," because so many cars have grazed the wall there.

Ever since Johnny Mantz started in last place and proceeded to win its inaugural race, the Southern 500, in 1950, Darlington has become one of NASCAR's favorite venues. "You never forget your first love," Dale Earnhardt once said in describing the odd oval, "whether it's a high-school sweetheart, a faithful old hunting dog, or a fickle racetrack in South Carolina with a contrary disposition. And, if you happen to be a race car driver, there's no victory so sweet, so memorable, as whipping Darlington Raceway."

The beloved landmark definitely lived up to its feisty legend during the 47th annual Carolina Dodge Dealers 400, the fifth race of the 2003 NASCAR season. Craven started the 293-lap contest in 31st place. Besides the built-in challenges at Darlington, the weather played a part, too. As the afternoon sun heated up, so did the track's asphalt surface. Tires soften and cars usually run faster on a hot track, and that's what happened with Craven's No. 32 Pontiac.

He had motored into fifth place with 70 laps left. At lap 268, the second- and third-place cars, driven by Elliott Sadler and Jeff Gordon, separately hit the wall—fresh victims of the Darlington stripe. Busch

Kurt Busch

zoomed up from behind in his No. 97 Ford and slipped below, then past them. Now the race became a door-to-door duel between Busch and Craven.

Craven, then 36 years old, was born in Maine and cut his stock car teeth on New England's regional NASCAR circuit. He won a rookie of the year award in the lower ranks before joining the top circuit in 1995. Coincidentally, his only other major victory came in a last-lap clash with Dale Jarrett in the 2001 Old Dominion 500 at Virginia's Martinsville Speedway.

Las Vegas native Busch had enjoyed considerable success before this dustup at Darlington. After cleaning up in several junior series, he made his big-time NASCAR debut in 2000, running in seven major events. At 23, the young gun grabbed headlines in 2002, winning four races, including three of the season's last five. He finished the year fourth in the standings, 159 points behind champion Tony Stewart.

So neither of these guys was bashful in the face of Darlington's untamed turf. Over the last two laps, there was lots of bumping and grinding as the duo jockeyed back and forth for first place. Busch's power steering had gone on the fritz with ten laps remaining, making his car feel "like it weighed 10,000 pounds in the corners," he later said.

Kurt Busch gives Ricky Craven a congratulatory hug after the two battled for first place at Darlington.

With one lap to go, Busch took a slight lead. As they barreled out of Turn 4, Craven moved to the inside of Busch's Ford, and the two started playing bumper cars. Their fenders were practically touching when they blazed across the line in a photo finish.

In a post-race interview, Craven recalled taking his cool-down lap, unaware of the results. "Did we win the race?" he asked his crew on the radio. "I came off of Turn 2, I looked up and it showed us first on the scoreboard. That was the confirmation." Ironically, Craven was credited for leading only one lap, although it was the one that counted most.

Busch talked about the high-speed exhilaration during the thrilling race's final seconds. "Coming to the line, I had my foot on the floor as hard as I could and I tried to hold the wheel as straight as I could," he said. "[Ricky] was running out of racetrack. I mean, the excitement level within the car—you have to block it out and you have to focus on what you have to do. There was so much going on. My arms were numb, my brain was numb."

Craven's reaction? "It's the most fun I've ever had in my life," he gushed. "This is exactly what you dream about, the perfect way to win at the perfect track."

TV Cameras Catch the Action

While there's nothing quite like attending a NASCAR race in person, sometimes the best seats in the house are in America's living rooms. Thanks to dozens of television cameras, viewers at home get to see every angle imaginable—even from right inside the race cars!

The 2002 Daytona 500 is a perfect example. NBC Sports used 68 cameras to cover the race from green flag to checkered flag. Nine cameras were set up around the grandstands. There were eight unmanned robotic cameras, including one mounted on the fence at each of the four turns. "Fan Cam" took crowd shots, "Flag Cam" was bolted to the top of the flagpole, and "Sky Cam" beamed images from a helicopter. Two cameras were set up inside the broadcast booth, two more were attached to long booms that stretched out over the track, and another two were used by roving reporters. There were 10 cameras mounted along pit road, plus four carried by roving operators. Finally, to capture the driver's-eye view, 10 cars each had three cameras inside: one for a front view, one for a rear view, and one for a side view. You can't get much closer than that!

82

Close, Closer, Closest

Here are the five closest finishes in NASCAR's top series since the current electronic timing and scoring system was instituted in 1993 (ranked by margin of victory in seconds):

.002 Ricky Craven beats Kurt Busch, Darlington Raceway, **March 16, 2003**

.005 Dale Earnhardt beats Ernie Irvan, Talladega Superspeedway, **July 25, 1993**

.006 Kevin Harvick beats Jeff Gordon, Atlanta Motor Speedway, **March 11, 2001**

.010 Dale Earnhardt beats Bobby Labonte, Atlanta Motor Speedway, **March 12, 2000**

.025 Jimmy Spencer beats Bill Elliott, Talladega Superspeedway, **July 24, 1994**